MUSIC IS MY THERAPY

MUSIC IS MY THERAPY

BY AUTHOR AND THERAPIST: *JENNIFER A. POPE, LCSW-C*

gatekeeper press™
Columbus, Ohio

Music Is My Therapy

Published by Gatekeeper Press
2167 Stringtown Rd, Suite 109
Columbus, OH 43123-2989
www.GatekeeperPress.com

ISBN (paperback): 9781662901683
eISBN: 9781662901676

This book is dedicated to:
My Amazing Parents
Alexander & Phyllis: the love and support you've given me cannot be measured...
Thank you for giving me the lens to dream in color, the wings to fly the skies
of possibility, and the confidence to know I can do ANYTHING!

Rest In Power Daddy, thank you for the love, the life, and the Music....

To My One and Only Sister
Kristen: How lucky am I that my parents blessed me with my very best
friend... Thank you for all that you are, all that you do, and the beauty
you add to our world; keep being awesome beyond measure!

To My Children
Jordan & Julian: You have given me a purpose to make this world better
than I found it. All that I do is to make you guys proud that I'm your
Mother. Know that you can achieve anything with hard work, dedication
and perseverance. There are no boundaries in my love for you.

TABLE OF CONTENTS

How to Use This Workbook

This workbook can be used independently or used with a therapist to assist in your treatment plan. Listen to the song suggestions for each chapter. You can also add some songs that you believe fit the chapter theme. Complete the sections for each chapter and use them to reflect and identify your personal feelings for each chapter theme. At the end of each chapter, select a song to personify your personal experience in the theme chapter. At the end of the workbook, use the list of songs you selected at the end of each chapter to create your own soundtrack to wellness. Create a playlist on your music player and enjoy!

All song suggestions can be found on music platforms such as: Apple Music, Spotify, Soundcloud, Youtube, Tidal, Spinrilla and more.

MUSIC & THE MIND:
HOW IT ALL WORKS?

Music activates every known part of the brain. Listening to and playing music can make you smarter, happier, healthier and more productive at all stages of life. (1) Music arouses emotion from the nucleus accumbens, a major player in the brain's reward circuit. The nucleus accumbens operate on two neurotransmitters: dopamine, which helps regulate emotional responses, and serotonin, which can affect mood and social behavior. This is why songs can instantly grab our emotions and transport us back to a certain time and place. Music improves brain function because of its ability to activate the array of neurons across the corpus collosum, creating a state of communicable harmony between the two hemispheres. The non-verbal melodies stimulate the right hemisphere while the singing stimulates the language center housed in our left brain. Music boosts endorphin release which in turn lifts our spirits and triggers positive emotional responses and senses of euphoria. (4) Music activates the same brain structures and regions linked to other euphoric stimuli, such as food, sex, and drugs. Blood rises and falls with the swells of music in areas of the brain associated with reward, emotion, and arousal. In addition, music activates the motor cortex, the part of the brain that controls voluntary movements. So, when you are tapping your foot, snapping your fingers, or bobbing your head to the beat of a song, you can thank your motor cortex.

Music also stimulates memories from the hippocampus, the center of memory, learning, and emotion located in the medial temporal lobe of the brain. This is why listening to a particular song can take you on a walk down memory lane and invoke the feeling of déjà vu. With the potential to alter an individual's conscious state, music therapy can shift an individual's perception of time and stimulate emotions and memories. (4)

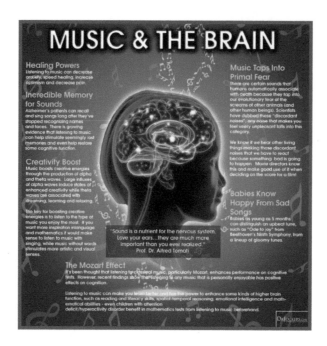

Picture from *https://drjockers.com/3-ways-music-improves-brain-function/*

Listening therapy, a highly specialized modality of mental health therapy, uses specifically modulated music to improve brain function. Listening therapy is often known as music therapy as well. As emotional/psychological trauma can affect the functions of the brain in multiple ways, listening therapy can restore brain function back to its pre-trauma state. The three areas of the brain that are impacted the most by emotional /psychological trauma are the amygdala, hippocampus, and prefrontal cortex. We know that music and language use the same neurological pathways. (3) Fortunately, the brain can change with appropriate input. This is called neuroplasticity. Yet, it doesn't happen with just one try. To create lasting change, input must be repeated over time to change neural networks. (3) The neural pathways for sound are improved and strengthened through neuroplasticity while also making new connections. (2) With proper input of beneficial sound, and repetition over time, one will see the various ways listening therapy improves brain function.

As we can appreciate music for its entertainment purposes, music is an underutilized tool for healing. Music releases dopamine in the reward center of the brain, the same chemical released when you eat your favorite food. This is also why finding new music you love is so exciting and you seem like you just can't get enough! Listening to pleasurable music releases dopamine, and dopamine increases happiness. People also love music because they can express their personalities and opinions through the music they listen to. So often we can relate song lyrics to experiences in our own lives. This workbook allows you to use music to creatively to make the link from the art to your life's experiences while highlighting how it assists in your mental wellness. Let us begin your journey to wellness…

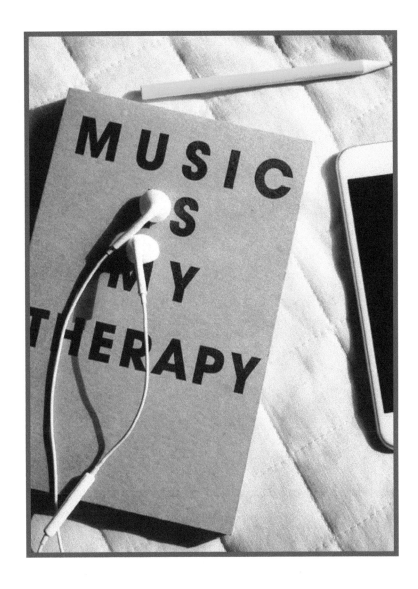

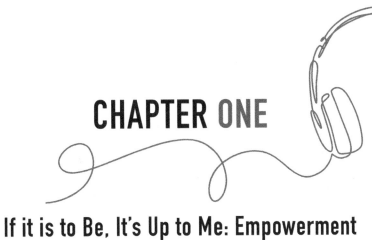

CHAPTER ONE

If it is to Be, It's Up to Me: Empowerment

Let's be empowered! The process of becoming stronger and more confident will help you to navigate and take control of your life, with the knowledge of your right to fulfill your purpose and to be ignited with profound lyrics over a deep felt rhythm. There are songs you hear that spark the power that drive you to be better, stronger, and filled with purpose. These are the songs you listen to in the morning as you drive to work, drink your morning coffee, write a challenging paper, or tackle that hard assignment. These songs remind us of who we are and what we have in us… Power!

Now Playing:

"I Believe" by Fantasia Burrino
"Level Up" by Ciara
"Roar" by Katie Perry
"Stronger (What Doesn't Kill You)" Kelli Clarkson
"Me, Myself and I" by G-Easy and Bebe Rexha
"Eye of the Tiger" by Survivor
"We Are the Champions" by Queen
"Respect" by Aretha Franklin
"Formation" by Beyonce
"Stand" by Donnie McClurkin
"Ventilation" by Nato Means
"You Should See Me in a Crown" by Billie Eilish
"Juice "by Lizzo
"Bitch Better Have My Money" by Rihanna

Impactful Song Lyric:

_____
_____
_____
_____
_____
_____
_____

How did it make you feel?

_____
_____
_____
_____
_____
_____
_____

How does it apply to YOUR life?

_____
_____
_____
_____
_____
_____
_____

What coping skill/ healing method does it provide you?

_____
_____
_____
_____
_____
_____
_____

Your Song for _EMPOWERMENT_: _____
_____

If it is to Be, it's up to Me: Empowerment

Impactful Lyrics:

_____

_____

_____

Song Title: _____

Artist: _____

Impactful Lyrics:

_____

_____

_____

Song Title: _____

Artist: _____

Impactful Lyrics:

_____

_____

_____

Song Title: _____

Artist: _____

Impactful Lyrics:

_____

_____

_____

Song Title: _____

Artist: _____

Impactful Lyrics:

_____

_____

_____

Song Title: _____

Artist: _____

CHAPTER TWO

I'm Mad: Anger & Frustration

Anger is one of our most natural and powerful emotions. Many people will urge you to suppress it; however, it's actually healthier to embrace it as it is channeled properly. Hitting the bag at the gym, running five miles, or doing a rapid moving task like typing are good examples. It's inevitable; at some point in life you will experience anger in one of its many forms. Surprisingly, anger can be good. It increases optimism, creativity, and effective performance. Actually, it may surprise you that anger can hurt you, too, so let's play it out....

Now Playing:

"Break Stuff" by Limp Bizkit
"Fuck the Police" by N.W.A.
"You Oughtta Know" by Alanis Morissette
"I Don't Give a Fuck" by Tupac
"Angry All the Time" by Tim McGraw
"Fuck You" by CeeLo Green
"Leave Me Alone" by Michael Jackson
"Caught out There" by Kelis
"Numb" by Linkin Park
"B.E.E.F." by Cypher DeVerdad
"Scream" by Michael Jackson & Janet Jackson
"Last Resort" by Papa Roach
"Ring the Alarm" by Beyonce
"I Don't Fuck with You" by Big Sean

Impactful Song Lyric:

_____
_____
_____
_____
_____
_____
_____

How did it make you feel?

_____
_____
_____
_____
_____
_____
_____
_____
_____

How does it apply to YOUR life?

_____
_____
_____
_____
_____
_____
_____
_____

What coping skill/ healing method does it provide you?

_____
_____
_____
_____
_____
_____
_____
_____

Your Song for _Anger & Frustration_:_____
_____

I'm Mad: Anger and Frustration

Impactful Lyrics:

_____
_____
_____

Song Title: _____
Artist: _____

Impactful Lyrics:

_____
_____
_____

Song Title: _____
Artist: _____

Impactful Lyrics:

_____
_____
_____

Song Title: _____
Artist: _____

Impactful Lyrics:

_____
_____
_____

Song Title: _____
Artist: _____

Impactful Lyrics:

_____
_____
_____

Song Title: _____
Artist: _____

CHAPTER THREE

Soothe the Soul: Reflection

Nothing soothes the soul like music melodies that are accompanied by lyrics that wrap you in a big auditory blanket of comfort and solace. The endorphins that our brains release while listening to soft jazz, relax our minds, and we begin to slow our breathing. Our heart rates decrease, and our physiology begins to do all the work. The magic of music is the massage of the mind that allows us to unwind. The melodic sounds of these songs are felt so deep, they often don't even need words.

Now Playing:
....

"Closer" by Goapele
"Stand by Me" by Ben E. King
"Wey U"by Chante Moore
"Angel" by Anita Baker
"Serendipity" by Easterly
"Cranes in the Sky" by Solange
"Cool" by Anthony Hamilton
"In a Sentimental Mood" by Duke Ellington & John Coltrane
"Be Thankful" by William DeVaughn
"Jahraymecofasola" by Jill Scott
"ManTime" by Ferrari Cash

Impactful Song Lyric:

_____
_____
_____
_____
_____
_____
_____

How did it make you feel?

_____
_____
_____
_____
_____
_____
_____

How does it apply to YOUR life?

_____
_____
_____
_____
_____
_____
_____

What coping skill/ healing method does it provide you?

_____
_____
_____
_____
_____
_____
_____
_____

Your Song for _Soul Reflection_: _____

_____

Soothe the Soul: Reflection

Impactful Lyrics:

_____

_____

_____

Song Title: _____

Artist: _____

Impactful Lyrics:

_____

_____

_____

Song Title: _____

Artist: _____

Impactful Lyrics:

_____

_____

_____

Song Title: _____

Artist: _____

Impactful Lyrics:

_____

_____

_____

Song Title: _____

Artist: _____

Impactful Lyrics:

_____

_____

_____

Song Title: _____

Artist: _____

CHAPTER FOUR

I Can't Stop Smiling: Love

Descriptions of love through song are one of love's most popular art forms. There are more songs about love than any other emotion in the world. It is transcribed in different cultures, different languages, and across all genres. There are some love songs that can describe exactly how you feel for someone, word for word, beat by beat. The songs convey a form of deep-felt happiness  that sometimes cannot be fully captured with just words alone. The many dynamics and dimensions of love can be felt deeply with the accompaniment of melodic sounds, perfect pitches, and voices that are termed as one of the many wonders of the world.

Now Playing:

"Love & Happiness" by Al Green
"Lovin' You" by Minnie Riperton
"The Power of Love" by Celine Dion
"Greatest Love of All" by Whitney Houston
"Endless Love" by Diana Ross & Lionel Richie
"Crash into Me" by Dave Matthews Band
"Cause I Love You" by Lenny Williams
"Love Calls" by Kem
"So Beautiful" by Musiq Soulchild
"How Do I Live" by Leanne Rimes
"Mirrors" by Justin Timberlake
"Came Here for Love" by Sigala and Ella Eyre

Impactful Song Lyric:

_____
_____
_____
_____
_____
_____
_____

How did it make you feel?

_____
_____
_____
_____
_____
_____
_____

How does it apply to YOUR life?

_____
_____
_____
_____
_____
_____
_____

What coping skill/ healing method does it provide you?

_____
_____
_____
_____
_____
_____
_____
_____

Your Song for _Love_ : _____
_____

I Can't Stop Smiling: Love

Impactful Lyrics:

_____
_____
_____

Song Title: _____
Artist: _____

Impactful Lyrics:

_____
_____
_____

Song Title: _____
Artist: _____

Impactful Lyrics:

_____
_____
_____

Song Title: _____
Artist: _____

Impactful Lyrics:

_____
_____
_____

Song Title: _____
Artist: _____

Impactful Lyrics:

_____
_____
_____

Song Title: _____
Artist: _____

CHAPTER FIVE

A Dream, Yes, I have It: Hope

Our hopes and dreams often come with a vision. We can actually see the achievement of the goal we believe we are destined to achieve. We often hear a song that motivates us to chase our dreams, to dream a dream, or to have an outlook of great aspirations and ambition. These songs give us an auditory "don't stop," "keep up the good work," "you're almost there, keep going" collective of sounds, beats, and rhythms that push us to our successes.

Now Playing:

"I know I Can" by Nas
"We Gon' Be Alright" by Kendrick Lamar
"Bridge over Troubled Water" by Simon and Garfunkel
"Believe" by Sounds of Blackness
"I Can See Clearly Now" by Johnny Nash
"We Love Music" by G. Hood
"Don't Stop Believin'" by Journey
"Never Give Up" by Yolanda Adams
"Somewhere Over the Rainbow" by Israel Kamakawiwo'ole
"Better Days" by Le'Andria Johnson
"Here Comes the Sun" by The Beatles
"Lean on Me" by Bill Withers
"Hold on, We're Going Home" by Drake

Impactful Song Lyric:

_____
_____
_____
_____
_____
_____
_____

How did it make you feel?

_____
_____
_____
_____
_____
_____
_____

How does it apply to YOUR life?

_____
_____
_____
_____
_____
_____
_____

What coping skill/ healing method does it provide you?

_____
_____
_____
_____
_____
_____
_____
_____

Your Song for _Hope_: _____
_____

A Dream, Yes, I have It: Hope

Impactful Lyrics:

_____

_____

_____

Song Title: _____

Artist: _____

Impactful Lyrics:

_____

_____

_____

Song Title: _____

Artist: _____

Impactful Lyrics:

_____

_____

_____

Song Title: _____

Artist: _____

Impactful Lyrics:

_____

_____

_____

Song Title: _____

Artist: _____

Impactful Lyrics:

_____

_____

_____

Song Title: _____

Artist: _____

CHAPTER SIX

Blue Blues: Sadness (Depression)

At times, sadness plagues us in life and can be paralyzing. We can experience sadness at normal levels, but sometimes the sadness lingers around and leads to depression. Although sadness is also a natural feeling, when it begins to affect our day-to-day life and becomes debilitating, it is time to seek professional help. Depression is often overlooked and under-addressed in our society, so much that it appears to be normal. Utilize a mental health professional to help differentiate between feeling sad and suffering from depression. Sadness is one of the biggest themes in music across all genres. Sometimes the only way to express this feeling is through music.

Now Playing:

"Charlene" by Anthony Hamilton
"I'm Going Down" by Mary J. Blige
"Gone" by NSync
"Back to Black" by Amy Winehouse
"Hear My Cry" by Jill Scott
"How You Remind Me" by Nickelback
"Someone to Love" by Queen
"Someone Like You" by Adele
"Ich bin der Welt abhanden gekommen" ("I've Become Lost to The World") by Gustav Mahler
"It Will Rain" by Bruno Mars
"Unchained Melody" by Righteous Brothers
"Dance with My Father" by Luther Vandross
"Feelings" by Floetry
"Wish You Were Here" by Pink Floyd

Impactful Song Lyric:

_____
_____
_____
_____
_____
_____
_____

How did it make you feel?

_____
_____
_____
_____
_____
_____
_____

How does it apply to YOUR life?

_____
_____
_____
_____
_____
_____
_____

What coping skill/ healing method does it provide you?

_____
_____
_____
_____
_____
_____
_____
_____

Your Song for _Sadness_: _____
_____

Blue Blues: Sadness (Depression)

Impactful Lyrics:

_____

_____

_____

Song Title: _____

Artist: _____

Impactful Lyrics:

_____

_____

_____

Song Title: _____

Artist: _____

Impactful Lyrics:

_____

_____

_____

Song Title: _____

Artist: _____

Impactful Lyrics:

_____

_____

_____

Song Title: _____

Artist: _____

Impactful Lyrics:

_____

_____

_____

Song Title: _____

Artist: _____

CHAPTER SEVEN

Prayer & Purpose: Spiritual Revelation

Spiritual revelation is the introspective gift from a God/Higher Power through divine spirit to observe and receive divine information of event or subject past, present and/or that is to come. It is the guide into the distinctive picture or position of God regarding certain issues or arrangements, either for individual or group purpose. Music can allow us to vibrate on higher levels of consciousness and elevate our spiritual awareness. Music resonates within the human spirit. At the heart of humanity is a song of the soul. The spiritual significance of music can transcend communities, cultures, and creeds. Music continues to inspire spiritual expression as sound reflects and affects faith and values. Beliefs and perceptions will transcend the very nature of music and lyrics.

Now Playing:
....

"Break Every Chain" by Tasha Cobbs
"Open My Heart" by Yolanda Adams
"Journey in Satchidananda" by Alice Coltrane feat. Pharoah Sanders
"When You Believe" by Mariah Carey and Whitney Houston
"Savior's Shadow" by Blake Shelton
"Hey God" by Bon Jovi
"Nobody Greater" by Vashawn Mitchell
"What If God Was One of Us?" by Joan Osborne
"You Found Me" by The Fray
"I Look to You" by Whitney Houston
"Take Me Higher" by The Clark Sisters
"Creator Has a Master Plan" by Pharoah Sanders

Impactful Song Lyric:

_____
_____
_____
_____
_____
_____
_____

How did it make you feel?

_____
_____
_____
_____
_____
_____
_____
_____

How does it apply to YOUR life?

_____
_____
_____
_____
_____
_____
_____
_____

What coping skill/ healing method does it provide you?

_____
_____
_____
_____
_____
_____
_____
_____

Your Song for _Spiritual Revelation_: _____
_____

Prayer & Purpose: Spiritual Revelation

Impactful Lyrics:

_____
_____
_____

Song Title: _____

Artist: _____

Impactful Lyrics:

_____
_____
_____

Song Title: _____

Artist: _____

Impactful Lyrics:

_____
_____
_____

Song Title: _____
Artist: _____

Impactful Lyrics:

_____
_____
_____

Song Title: _____
Artist: _____

Impactful Lyrics:

_____
_____
_____

Song Title: _____
Artist: _____

CHAPTER **EIGHT**

Man, I Feel Like a Woman: Self-Confidence (Women)

Often times this world can seem so harsh, especially as a woman. Women are the backbone of our families, the nucleus of our communities and most importantly, the givers of life! And with all that power, it seems the world can sometimes shrink women into being an afterthought, fragile and too delicate, and overly emotional. The negative connotations have too often resulted  in women's low self-esteem and second guessing their worth. But for every negative generalization placed upon women, there is a song that will make them feel powerful, worthy, unstoppable, and confident to be exactly what they are……. MAGIC!

Now Playing:
....

"Run the World" by Beyoncé
"Feel Like A Woman" by Shania Twain
"Womanfesto" by Jill Scott
"Electric Lady" by Janelle Monaè
"I'm Every Woman" by Chaka Khan
"Respect" by Aretha Franklin
"Girl on Fire" by Alicia Keys
"Born this Way" by Lady Gaga
"Just a Girl" by No Doubt
"U.N.I.T.Y." by Queen Latifah
"God Is a Woman" by Ariana Grande
"Juice" by Lizzo

Impactful Song Lyric:

_____
_____
_____
_____
_____
_____
_____

How did it make you feel?

_____
_____
_____
_____
_____
_____
_____

How does it apply to YOUR life?

_____
_____
_____
_____
_____
_____
_____

What coping skill/ healing method does it provide you?

_____
_____
_____
_____
_____
_____
_____

Your Song for _Self-Confidence (Women)_: _____
_____

Man, I Feel Like a Woman: Self Confidence (Women)

Impactful Lyrics:

_____

_____

_____

Song Title: _____

Artist: _____

Impactful Lyrics:

_____

_____

_____

Song Title: _____

Artist: _____

Impactful Lyrics:

_____

_____

_____

Song Title: _____

Artist: _____

Impactful Lyrics:

_____

_____

_____

Song Title: _____

Artist: _____

Impactful Lyrics:

_____

_____

_____

Song Title: _____

Artist: _____

CHAPTER NINE

King of Kings: Self-Confidence (Men)

The terms "male empowerment" and "male self-confidence" are almost nonexistent. The world truly believes men are naturally equipped with built-in self-confidence to sustain themselves through all of the challenges being upstanding, respectable, and impactful men. Although being a man isn't always easy, being a good man is an art form. If you›ve mastered the fine art of masculinity by being one of the good guys, there is no doubt you have a soundtrack of songs that fuels your self-confidence.

Now Playing:

"Sabotage" by Beastie Boys
"Eye of the Tiger" by Survivor
"Don't Stop Me Now" by Queen
"Can't Hold Us" by Macklamore and Ryan Lewis
"Me, Myself, & I" by G-Eazy & Bebe Rexha
"Radioactive" by Imagine Dragons
"Man in the Mirror" by Michael Jackson
"With Arms Wide Open" by Creed
"One Man Can Change the World" by Big Sean, Kanye West and John Legend
"Better Man" by Leon Bridges
"It's a Man's World" by James Brown
"My Guy" by Mary Wells
"Whatta Man" by Salt N Peppa
"The Truth" by India Arie

Impactful Song Lyric:

_____
_____
_____
_____
_____
_____

How did it make you feel?

_____
_____
_____
_____
_____
_____

How does it apply to YOUR life?

_____
_____
_____
_____
_____
_____

What coping skill/ healing method does it provide you?

_____
_____
_____
_____
_____
_____

Your Song for _Self-Confidence (Men)_: _____
_____

King of Kings: Self-Confidence (Men)

Impactful Lyrics:

_____

_____

_____

Song Title: _____

Artist: _____

Impactful Lyrics:

_____

_____

_____

Song Title: _____

Artist: _____

Impactful Lyrics:

_____

_____

_____

Song Title: _____

Artist: _____

Impactful Lyrics:

_____

_____

_____

Song Title: _____

Artist: _____

Impactful Lyrics:

_____

_____

_____

Song Title: _____

Artist: _____

CHAPTER TEN

I am Me: Self-Awareness

Self-awareness allows you to create what you want and begin the journey of mastering your life. Self-awareness allows you to figure out where you focus your attention: your emotions, reactions, personality and behavior determine where you go in life. It gives you a clear perception of your personality, including strengths, weaknesses, thoughts, beliefs, motivation, and emotions. What better tool to use to tap into and focus your energies in self-awareness than music?

Now Playing:

"On and On" by Erykah Badu
"Scars to Your Beautiful" by Alessia Cara
"I Need to Move On" by Alex Lahey
"Bodak Yellow" by Cardi B
"Breathe" by Umi
"B.S." by Jhené Aiko feat H.E.R.
"Royals" by Lorde
"Find Yourself" by Great Good Fine Ok & Before You Exit
"What's My Name" by Snoop Dogg
"Shea Butter Baby" by Ari Lennox & J. Cole
"Enjoy Your Life" by Marina
"Soulmate" by Lizzo
"Papa's Got a Brand New Bag" by James Brown

Impactful Song Lyric:

_____
_____
_____
_____
_____
_____
_____

How did it make you feel?

_____
_____
_____
_____
_____
_____
_____

How does it apply to YOUR life?

_____
_____
_____
_____
_____
_____
_____

What coping skill/ healing method does it provide you?

_____
_____
_____
_____
_____
_____
_____

Your Song for _Self-Awareness:_ _____
_____

I am Me: Self-Awareness

Impactful Lyrics:

_____

_____

_____

Song Title: _____

Artist: _____

Impactful Lyrics:

_____

_____

_____

Song Title: _____

Artist: _____

Impactful Lyrics:

_____

_____

_____

Song Title: _____

Artist: _____

Impactful Lyrics:

_____

_____

_____

Song Title: _____

Artist: _____

Impactful Lyrics:

_____

_____

_____

Song Title: _____

Artist: _____

CHAPTER ELEVEN

Work It Out: Physical Health

Music and dance together seem to create an emotional quotient, always complementing each other. Music and dance create the perfect formula for release and self-expression. Music, be it a lullaby sung to a baby in a cradle or a soldier with his gun marching in a parade, can make you dance. We can also see that music can produce emotions and that emotions can find an outlet in dancing.

Now Playing:

"Turn Up the Music" by Chris Brown
"Party Rock Anthem" by LMAFO
"Y'all Get Back Now" by Big Freeda
"Uptown Funk" by Bruno Mars & Mark Ranson
"Push It" by Salt-N-Pepa
"Workout Plan" by Kanye West
"Play Hard" by David Guetta
"Suit and Tie" by Justin Timberlake
"Gangnam Style" by Psy
"Bootylicious" by Destiny's Child

Impactful Song Lyric:

_____

_____

_____

_____

_____

_____

How did it make you feel?

_____

_____

_____

_____

_____

_____

How does it apply to YOUR life?

_____

_____

_____

_____

_____

_____

What coping skill/ healing method does it provide you?

_____

_____

_____

_____

_____

_____

Your Song for _Physical Wellness_: _____

_____

Work It Out: Physical Wellness

Impactful Lyrics:

_____
_____
_____

Song Title: _____
Artist: _____

Impactful Lyrics:

_____
_____
_____

Song Title: _____
Artist: _____

Impactful Lyrics:

_____
_____
_____

Song Title: _____
Artist: _____

Impactful Lyrics:

_____
_____
_____

Song Title: _____
Artist: _____

Impactful Lyrics:

_____
_____
_____

Song Title: _____
Artist: _____

CHAPTER TWELVE

Power, Passion, Purpose: Self-Motivation

Who better to motivate you to reach your goals but YOU?! Self-motivation is one of the main deciding factors of success. Knowing that you have the drive, resiliency, vision, and perseverance to overcome any obstacle, and break any barrier, and to achieve your dreams is one of the greatest gifts. Songs that remind you of your determination to not only be great but better than great. This level of self-determination comes from within. These songs help bring it to the forefront to make you remember who you are, a WINNER!

Now Playing:

"I'm a Boss" by Rick Ross
"Everybody Mad" by OT Genesis
"Hustle and Motivate" by Nipsey Hussle
"Survivor" by Destiny's Child
"Stronger" by Britney Spears
"The Show Must Go On" by Queen
"I Feel Good" by James Brown
"Lose Yourself" by Eminem
"Heal the World" by Michael Jackson
"Get Up Stand Up" by Bob Marley
"Don't Stop Believin'" by Journey

Impactful Song Lyric:

_____
_____
_____
_____
_____
_____
_____

How did it make you feel?

_____
_____
_____
_____
_____
_____
_____

How does it apply to YOUR life?

_____
_____
_____
_____
_____
_____
_____

What coping skill/ healing method does it provide you?

_____
_____
_____
_____
_____
_____
_____

Your Song for _Self-Motivation_: _____
_____

Power, Passion, Purpose: Self-Motivation

Impactful Lyrics:

_____

_____

_____

Song Title: _____

Artist: _____

Impactful Lyrics:

_____

_____

_____

Song Title: _____

Artist: _____

Impactful Lyrics:

_____

_____

_____

Song Title: _____

Artist: _____

Impactful Lyrics:

_____

_____

_____

Song Title: _____

Artist: _____

Impactful Lyrics:

_____

_____

_____

Song Title: _____

Artist: _____

CHAPTER THIRTEEN

Your Soundtrack (Your 12-track playlist)

Choose one song from each chapter to create your own life soundtrack. These songs should hold a very personal meaning to your feelings, your experiences, and your life perceptions. They can be songs that represent your current life, a way of being that you've grown from, or even what you dream of being. Allow this soundtrack to reflect your personal journey through this fasci-  nating thing we call life. Reflect on its beauty, its triumphs, its challenges, and its ability to create the most beautiful and unique masterpiece, YOU!

1._____
2._____
3._____
4._____
5._____
6._____
7._____
8._____
9._____
10._____
11._____
12._____

You have now composed the unique and creative soundtrack of you! It is a masterpiece like no other. Add this playlist on your smart phone, tablet, or laptop and enjoy.

MUSIC QUOTES

"I still believe in the things I can't see... I believe in the things I can feel: Music, Love, and God."
—Lina Loy

"Again, when the mind is doubtful, when the mind drinks deep of doubt-poison, the senses have no capacity to inject faith into the mind. Here also music comes to the rescue."
—Shri Chinmoy

"Beautiful music is the art of the prophets that can calm the agitations of the soul; it is one of the most magnificent and delightful presents God has given us."
—Martin Luther

"Music is the easiest method of meditation. Whoever can let himself dissolve into music has no need to seek anything else to dissolve into."
—Osho

"Music should be healing; music should uplift the soul; music should inspire. There is no better way of getting closer to God, of rising higher towards the spirit, of attaining spiritual perfection than music, if only it is rightly understood."
—Hazrat Inayat Khan

"Music cleanses the understanding, inspires it, and lifts it into a realm which it could not reach if it were left to itself."
—Henry War Beecher

"One good thing about music, when it hits you, you feel no pain."
—Bob Marley

"If music be the food of love, play on, Give me excess of it; that surfeiting, The appetite may sicken, and so die."
—William Shakespeare

that which cannot be said and on which it is impossible to be silent."

...uches us emotionally, where words alone can't."
...ay Depp

...Music is the strongest form of magic."
—Marilyn Manson

"Music in the soul can be heard by the universe."
—Lao Tzu

Create your own Music Quote: _____
_____
_____
_____
_____

30 Day Music Therapy Challenge

MY GOAL:

WEEK'S REWARD:

MON	TUE	WED	THU	FRI	SAT	SUN
1. Karaoke Song	2. Feel Like A Badass Song	3. Feels Like Summertime Song	4. Morning Motivation Song	5. Song Dedicated To Your Ex Song	6. Love Of Your Life Song	7. Song In The Shower Song
8. Movie Soundtrack Song	9. Makes You Cry Song	10. Personal Anthem Song	11. Unpopular Favorite Song	12. Reminds You Of High School Song	13. Instrumental Song	14. Worst Day Of Your Life Song
15. Workout Song	16. All Time Favorite Song	17. Makes Me Want To Dance Song	18. Locker room Game Day Song	19. Never Want To Hear Again Song	20. Song Over 30 Years Old Song	21. Bath Time Decompress Song
22. New Love Song	23. Get Over A Break Up Song	24. Embarrassed I Like This Song	25. Crew Love Song	26. Road Trip Song	27. Favorite Song From The 80's Song	28. Favorite Disney Song
29. Broken-hearted Song	30. At Peace/Tranquil Song					

Special Thank You:

MikeLove MadeIt for making my vision come to life through his artistry.
www.mikelovemadeit.com IG: @mikelovemadeit

WORKS CITATIONS

1. Tseng P-T, Chen Y-W, Lin P-Y, et al. Significant treatment effect of adjunct music therapy to standard treatment on the positive, negative, and mood symptoms of schizophrenic patients: a meta-analysis. BMC Psychiatry. 2016;16:16. (Referenced in the first two sentences of "Music and the Brain.")
2. The ahttps://stemtalk.wixsite.com/stem-talk/single-post/2018/04/25/A-Musician's-Mind-and-the-Alternate-Uses-of-Music-Listening-to-music-affects-brain-structure-and-creativity-a-look-on-music-therapy
3. https://integratedlistening.com/what-is-listening-therapy/
4. https://drjockers.com/3-ways-music-improves-brain-function/ (Photo referenced in "Music and the Brain.")
5. Chapter pictures from https://www.pexels.com (Free Downloads)

Notes

Notes

Notes

Notes